SINGLE LINES OF PROSE AND QUOTES EXPLORING LIFE ONE LINE AT THE TIME

BY KRISTINA ALAVANJA

Today
is a
NEW
beginning

WELCOME TO THE STORY BEHIND THE BOOK COVER

The cover of this book is a visual invitation to embark on a journey of self-discovery and personal growth. It features an image of a person's hands resting on an open notebook, symbolizing the act of writing and the power of words. The phrase *"Your life, your prose" your Quote* is prominently displayed, serving as a reminder that we are all authors of our own lives and that the prose/Quotes within this book can become a part of your life.

Surrounding the notebook are various objects that add to the atmosphere of creativity and inspiration. A cup of tea and pieces of chocolate suggest comfort and indulgence, inviting the reader to take a moment for themselves. Dried flowers and an envelope with a visible red wax seal add a touch of nostalgia, evoking the enduring appeal of personal reflection and introspection.

This cover was chosen because it aligns well with the theme of the book - motivational, inspirational prose about life. It suggests that the contents of the book will inspire you to reflect on your own life, motivate you to pursue your dreams, and encourage you to write your own story.

I hope that this cover, like the **prose** within, will **inspire** and **motivate** you on your journey through life. So, dear reader, as you turn the pages of this book, may you find the inspiration you seek, the wisdom you need, and the courage to be who you truly are. Enjoy the journey of exploring life one line at a time! there's always something to learn, something to appreciate, and something to aspire to.

INTRODUCTION

Welcome to "Single Lines of Prose and Quotes: Exploring Life One Line at A Time". This book is not just a collection of words, but a journey through the various aspects of life, captured in single lines of prose and quotes.

In this book, prose is used to express thoughts and reflections in a straightforward and direct manner. For example, consider the line from the chapter "The Power of Can": "If you know how to say, I can't I am sure you know how to say I can." This line, though brief, conveys a powerful message about self-belief and potential.

Quotes, on the other hand, are typically brief and catchy statements that express an important idea or concept. An example from the book is, "To be who you want to be, you need to work on it, despite all the…" from the chapter "The Pursuit of Self". This quote encapsulates the essence of personal growth and self-improvement.

Each line, whether it's a piece of prose or a quote, offers its own unique insight and value. They are here to inspire, provoke thought, and stir the soul. They are not just to be read, but to be experienced. They are simple yet profound, brief yet impactful. They are the echoes of life's lessons, the whispers of wisdom, and the voice of experience.

Whether you're looking for inspiration, seeking solace, or simply wanting to view life from a different perspective, this book is for you. It's a reminder that no matter where you are in your journey,

AUTHOR'S NOTE

In this book, you will also find a selection of quotes from renowned individuals, whose words have resonated with me and inspired countless others. These quotes have been carefully chosen and included to enrich the tapestry of wisdom this book aims to present.

As the author, I have also contributed my own original prose and quotes, drawn from my personal experiences and insights. Each line I've written is a testament to the journey of life, capturing its various shades and nuances.

As you navigate through these pages, my hope is that these lines will inspire you, provoke thought, and stir your soul. They are not just to be read, but to be experienced. May they serve as sparks of insight, guiding lights in moments of uncertainty, and sources of comfort when you need it most.

So, embark on this journey of exploration and self-discovery, and may you find the inspiration you seek, the wisdom you need, and the courage to be who you truly are. Enjoy the journey of exploring life one line at a time!

Say yes to new
adventures

THE PURSUIT OF SELF

"To be who you want to be, you need to work on it, despite all the obstacles. It's a journey of self-discovery, of understanding your strengths and weaknesses, and learning to leverage them to your advantage. It's about not just surviving, but thriving in the face of adversity, and turning challenges into opportunities for growth. It's about embracing change, persisting through setbacks, and always striving to be the best version of yourself. Remember, the pursuit of self is not a destination, but a continuous journey."

LIVING IN THE MOMENT

"To appreciate the moment, you have to be in the moment. It's about fully immersing yourself in the present, letting go of past regrets and future anxieties. It's about focusing on the here and now, taking in the sights, sounds, and feelings that surround you. It's about finding joy in the simple things, and understanding that every moment is fleeting and unique. So, take a deep breath, clear your mind, and truly live in the moment. Because life isn't a destination, it's a journey, and every moment is a precious step along the way."

THE QUESTION OF EXISTANCE

"To be or not to be, that is the question that you have to answer yourself. It's a question that delves into the very core of our being, a philosophical conundrum that has puzzled thinkers for centuries. It's about making conscious choices, about deciding who you want to be and how you want to live your life. It's about understanding that existence is not merely about physical presence, but about the impact we make, the lives we touch, and the legacy we leave behind. So, ponder on this question, for the answer will shape not just your existence, but your essence."

LOST AND FOUND

"When you lose your compass, you lose yourself. But in the process of being lost, you often discover parts of yourself that were previously hidden, waiting to be found. It's a journey of self-discovery, a voyage into the unknown. It's about embracing the uncertainty, the fear, the confusion, and finding strength in vulnerability. It's about realizing that sometimes, you need to lose yourself to find yourself. We all experience a feeling of getting lost, but in time, with taking time for yourself and reflecting, you will find the cause of it and the cure for it.

THE JOURNEY TO SELF- LOVE

To be able to say, 'I love who I am,' you need to accept all your flaws. It's about embracing every part of yourself, the strengths and the weaknesses, the successes and the failures. It's about understanding that you are a work in progress and that every flaw is a part of your unique tapestry. It's about forgiving yourself for your mistakes and celebrating your victories. Self-love is not easy, it's hard work. It's like a fight with yourself, but once you accept your flaws as something beautiful and part of you, you will stop fighting and start loving. It's about realizing that self-love isn't about perfection, but about acceptance.

THE COURAGE IN DEAFEAT

"To admit defeat, it does not make you weak, it makes you courageous. It's about understanding that strength isn't just about winning, but also about knowing when to accept defeat. It's about recognizing that every setback is an opportunity to learn and grow. It's about realizing that courage isn't just about standing tall in victory, but also about standing up again after a fall. It's about acknowledging that sometimes, the bravest thing you can do is to admit defeat, learn from it, and move forward. So, remember, in every defeat, there is a hidden victory, and that is the courage to continue."

THE VALUE OF TRYING

"If you never in your life have said, 'I have tried,' that means that you have not lived. To try is to learn and grow. It's about stepping out of your comfort zone and daring to venture into the unknown. It's about embracing the possibility of failure as a stepping stone to success. It's about understanding that every attempt, every effort, no matter how small, brings you one step closer to your goals. It's about realizing that the value of trying lies not in the outcome, but in the journey, in the lessons learned, and in the person, you become along the way. So, dare to try, for to try is to truly live."

THE CREATION OF HAPPINESS

Happiness is what you create, not what you wait for. It's about understanding that happiness doesn't just happen, it's a choice that you make every day. It's about finding joy in the little things, and appreciating what you have while striving for what you want. It's about cultivating positivity, nurturing relationships, and investing in experiences that bring you joy. It's about realizing that waiting for happiness to come to you is like waiting for a ship at the airport. So, take charge, create your own happiness, because life is too short to wait for happiness to find you."

WALKING TOWARDS GOALS

"To reach towards your goals, you need to move your legs and walk towards it. Nothing will happen if you just stand and wish it. It's about understanding that goals aren't achieved through mere desire, but through action. It's about taking the first step, no matter how small, and continuing to move forward, no matter how difficult the journey. It's about perseverance, determination, and the will to overcome obstacles. It's about realizing that every step you take, no matter how small, brings you closer to your goals. So, don't just stand and wish, start walking towards your goals, because the journey of a thousand miles begins with a single step."

LEARNING FROM LIFE

"You don't always need to understand why this has happened. All you need to do is learn from it. It's about embracing the uncertainty of life, accepting that not everything happens for a reason that we can immediately understand. It's about finding the lessons in every experience, good or bad, and using them to grow and evolve. It's about realizing that life is the greatest teacher, and every experience is a lesson. It's about understanding that the wisdom of life lies not in understanding everything, but in learning from everything. So, when life throws you a curveball, don't waste time asking why. Instead, ask what you can learn from it."

THE RIGHT PATH

"Do what is right, not what is easy, because doing the right thing is not easy. It's about understanding that the path of righteousness often comes with challenges and obstacles. It's about making decisions not based on convenience, but on principles. It's about standing up for what you believe in, even when it's unpopular or difficult. It's about realizing that the easy path may be tempting, but the right path, though steep and rocky, leads to true fulfillment and peace. So, when faced with a choice, choose not what is easy, but what is right, because the value of a decision lies not in its ease, but in its integrity."

FRIENDSHIP WITH SELF

"Be your own best friend, before you become someone else's friend. It's about understanding that self-love and self-acceptance are the foundations of any healthy relationship. It's about treating yourself with the same kindness, respect, and understanding that you would offer to a dear friend. It's about celebrating your achievements, forgiving your mistakes, and encouraging your endeavours. It's about realizing that you cannot pour from an empty cup, and that to be a good friend to others, you first need to be a good friend to yourself. So, take the time to get to know yourself, to appreciate your uniqueness, and to cultivate a friendship with the person you spend the most time with - yourself."

THE THREE PILARS OF LIFE

"Throughout your lifespan, things will happen, life will change you, just never forget 3 things: where you came from, who you are, and who you want to be. It's about understanding that your past, present, and future form the three pillars of your life. Your past, where you came from, shapes your identity and values. Your present, who you are, reflects your current beliefs and actions. Your future, who you want to be, guides your growth and aspirations. It's about realizing that while life changes you, these three pillars remain constant. They ground you in your journey, providing a sense of continuity and direction. Remember your roots, be true to yourself, and keep sight of your dreams."

CREATING YOUR OWN TIME

"Stop waiting for the perfect time, the perfect time does not exist, create your own story here and now. It's about understanding that life doesn't come with a script, and that every moment is an opportunity to write your own narrative. It's about seizing the day, making the most of the present, and shaping your future. It's about realizing that waiting for the perfect time often means waiting forever. The perfect time is a myth, a mirage that keeps you from taking action. So, stop waiting, start doing. Create your own story, your own time, here and now. Because life isn't about waiting for the perfect moment, it's about creating it."

THE JOY OF SELF-CONTENTMENT

The Joy of Self-Contentment" celebrates the peace that comes from making choices that align with our values. The quote emphasizes the satisfaction of ending the day feeling good about ourselves and our decisions. It's about recognizing our worth, living authentically, and finding joy in our own contentment. Furthermore, it underscores the importance of self-love and authenticity. It's about understanding that our worth is not defined by external factors, but by our own self-perception and the choices we make. It's a celebration of the peace and satisfaction that comes from living true to ourselves, making decisions that resonate with our values, and embracing our unique journey with joy and contentment.

THE PATH OF RESILIENCE

"The Path of Resilience" symbolizes the journey of overcoming life's challenges. The quote emphasizes that resilience is about enduring hardships, symbolized by "painful rocks", with the knowledge that stability awaits. It's about-facing obstacles, learning from them, and emerging stronger. This path, though rocky, leads to growth and peace, celebrating our ability to adapt and persevere. It's a testament to our inner strength and resilience. Furthermore, it underscores the importance of faith and perseverance. It's about trusting in our ability to navigate through the rocky terrain, and believing in the promise of stability and peace at the end. It's a journey that shapes us, strengthens us, and ultimately, defines us

LIVING TODAY, WRITING TOMMOROW

"Living Today, Writing Tomorrow" is a powerful concept that emphasizes the importance of living in the present while shaping our future. The quote "Your tomorrow hasn't been written yet, your today has, live it" beautifully encapsulates this idea. It's about understanding that while our past and present are already written, our future is still a blank page. It's up to us to decide what we want to write on it. Every action we take today contributes to the story we'll tell tomorrow. However, it's equally important to not get so caught up in writing our future that we forget to live our present. Each day is a gift, and it's important to fully experience and appreciate it. After all, the moments we live today will become the memories of tomorrow.

THE DUAL NATURE OF LOSS

"The Dual Nature of Loss: 'You never lose, there are two ways that you benefit, when you win, you learn, when you lose, you learn. It's all about perception.'" This phrase is not just about winning or losing, but about the valuable lessons we gain from both. It's about understanding that even in loss, there's a win - the win of gaining knowledge and experience. This perspective transforms the concept of loss from a negative outcome to a stepping stone for growth. It's a testament to the resilience of the human spirit and the power of a positive mindset. It's a reminder that every outcome, win or lose, brings with it the opportunity to learn and grow. It's indeed a powerful way to navigate through life's challenges.

DREAMS AND REALITY

"Dreams and Reality: Dreaming won't give you what you want, it feeds the soul, but not the mouth." This phrase is not just about the contrast between dreams and reality, but also about the different needs they fulfill. It's about understanding that while dreams nourish our soul and inspire us, they don't necessarily satisfy our practical needs. This perspective highlights the importance of balancing our dreams with action. It's a testament to the need for hard work and practicality in achieving our dreams. It's a reminder that while dreaming is essential for inspiration and motivation, turning these dreams into reality requires action and effort. It's indeed a profound insight into the dual nature of dreams and reality.

LIFE: THE UNWRITTEN BOOK

"Life: The Unwritten Book: 'There is no book that can tell you about life, you need to live your life to know about it.'" This phrase is not just about the uniqueness of each individual's life, but also about the experiential knowledge that comes from living. It's about understanding that life cannot be fully comprehended through written words alone, but through personal experiences. This perspective emphasizes the importance of living fully and learning from our own journey. It's a testament to the richness of life's lessons that can't be captured in any book. It's a reminder that while books can guide us, the true essence of life is discovered through living. It's indeed a profound reflection on the nature of life and learning.

THE STRENGTH PAIN

"Strength in Pain: 'Turn your pain into strength, if you want to survive.'" is a potent concept that emphasizes the transformative power of pain. The quote "Turn your pain into strength, if you want to survive" beautifully encapsulates this idea. It's about understanding that while our past pains are already experienced, our future strength is yet to be built. It's up to us to decide how we transform our pain into strength. Every challenge we overcome today contributes to the resilience we'll display tomorrow. However, it's equally important to not get so consumed by our pain that we forget to acknowledge our growth. Each struggle is a lesson, and it's important to fully understand and appreciate it. After all, the trials we endure today will become the triumphs of tomorrow.

THE POWER OF PERSISTANCE

"The Power of Persistence: 'If you don't succeed once, keep trying until you do.'" is a compelling concept that underscores the importance of tenacity and determination. The quote "If you don't succeed once, keep trying until you do" perfectly embodies this idea. It's about understanding that while we may face setbacks and failures, our future success is still unwritten. It's up to us to keep trying and not give up. Every attempt we make today, successful or not, contributes to our journey towards success. However, it's equally important to not get so disheartened by failure that we stop trying. Each attempt is a step forward, and it's important to recognize and appreciate it

REGRET AND OPPORTUNITY

"Regret and Opportunity: 'Regret the missed opportunities, not the failures.'" is a profound concept that highlights the value of opportunities and the lessons learned from failures. The quote "Regret the missed opportunities, not the failures" perfectly encapsulates this idea. It's about understanding that while we may regret the opportunities we missed, our future is still full of potential. It's up to us to seize these opportunities and learn from our failures. Every opportunity we take today, successful or not, contributes to our journey towards success. However, it's equally important to not dwell on our failures but to see them as learning experiences

SWIMMING THROUGH LIFE'S STORMS

"Swimming Through Life's Storms: 'Stay strong and learn to swim, for life will throw many storms your way.'" is a powerful concept that emphasizes resilience and adaptability in the face of life's challenges. The quote "Stay strong and learn to swim, for life will throw many storms your way" perfectly encapsulates this idea. It's about understanding that life is full of challenges, akin to storms, and it's up to us to learn how to navigate through them. Every challenge we face and overcome today, strengthens our ability to handle future storms. However, it's equally important to not let these storms overwhelm us, but to see them as opportunities for growth and learning.

THE ART OF EMPATHY

"The Art of Empathy: 'Always put yourself in someone else's shoes before you decide to Judge.'" is a profound concept that emphasizes the importance of empathy and understanding in our interactions with others. The quote "Always put yourself in someone else's shoes before you decide to Judge" perfectly encapsulates this idea. It's about understanding that to truly comprehend someone's actions or decisions, we must try to see things from their perspective. Every time we practice empathy today, we enhance our ability to understand and connect with others. However, it's equally important to not let our judgments cloud our understanding, but to strive for empathy and compassion.

BREAKING FREE FROM THE PAST

"Breaking Free from the Past: 'You're not a prisoner of your own past, there is no lock and key. Leave it behind, learn from it, and move forward.'" is a liberating concept that emphasizes the ability to overcome past experiences and move forward. The quote "You're not a prisoner of your own past, there is no lock and key. Leave it behind, learn from it, and move forward" perfectly encapsulates this idea. It's about understanding that our past does not define us, and we have the power to break free from it. Every step we take towards overcoming our past today, contributes to our journey towards a brighter future. However, it's equally important to not let our past hold us back, but to learn from it and use it as a stepping stone towards growth

THE POWER OF PROGRESS

"The Power of Progress: 'With every step, you make progress. Focus on that, not on how slow it moves. Small steps can lead to big success.'" is an inspiring concept that emphasizes the importance of persistence and patience in our journey towards success. The quote "With every step, you make progress. Focus on that, not on how slow it moves. Small steps can lead to big success" perfectly encapsulates this idea. It's about understanding that progress is not always about speed, but about consistent effort and determination. Every step we take today, no matter how small, contributes to our journey towards success. However, it's equally important to not get disheartened by the pace of progress, but to appreciate each step forward.

THE INFLUENCE OF ACTIONS

The Influence of Actions: 'Every action we take shapes our identity and influences how we are perceived by others.'" is a profound concept that emphasizes the impact of our actions on our self-image and how others perceive us. The quote "Every action we take shapes our identity and influences how we are perceived by others" perfectly encapsulates this idea. It's about understanding that our actions, big or small, have a lasting impact on our identity and the impressions we leave on others. Every action we take today, consciously or unconsciously, contributes to the narrative of who we are. However, it's equally important to not let our past actions define us.

THE ART OF LISTENING

"The Art of Listening: 'Don't just listen, truly hear. Because to hear is to understand, to empathize, and ultimately, to care.'" is a profound concept that emphasizes the importance of active listening in our interactions with others. The quote "Don't just listen, truly hear. Because to hear is to understand, to empathize, and ultimately, to care" perfectly encapsulates this idea. It's about understanding that listening goes beyond just hearing words, it involves understanding the emotions and intentions behind them. Every conversation we engage in today, where we truly listen, contributes to our ability to understand, empathize, and care for others. However, it's equally important to not just passively hear, but to actively listen and understand.

FINDING LIFE'S PURPOSE

"Finding Life's Purpose: 'Find your life purpose and live it, your life will become more meaningful and you became happier and at peace.'" is a profound concept that emphasizes the importance of discovering and living our life's purpose. The quote "Find your life purpose and live it, your life will become more meaningful and you became happier and at peace" perfectly encapsulates this idea. It's about understanding that finding and living our life's purpose can bring a deeper sense of meaning, happiness, and peace to our lives. Every step we take towards discovering and living our purpose today, contributes to a more fulfilling and contented life. However, it's equally important to not let the search for purpose overwhelm us, but to embrace the journey with openness and curiosity

LIVING BY YOUR OWN RULES

"Living by Your Own Rules" means living authentically, guided by our own values and principles. Our lives are our own, and we have the right to live by our own rules. This brings authenticity and courage to our lives. However, it's important to remember that living by our own rules doesn't exempt us from following the law. Laws are societal rules that we must abide by for the safety and well-being of ourselves and others. We also exist in a world of connections. We must consider the impact of our actions on others. Living by our own rules doesn't mean disregarding others' rights and feelings It's about responsibility and adaptability, understanding that our 'rules' should evolve as we grow and learn. Remember, while we have the freedom to live by our own rules, we also have the responsibility to respect the rules of law and society

.

THE POWER OF CAN

"The Power of Can: 'If you know how to say, I can't I am sure you know how to say I can.'" This empowering statement emphasizes the importance of positive thinking and self-belief. The quote "If you know how to say, I can't I am sure you know how to say I can" perfectly encapsulates this idea. It's about understanding that the power to achieve lies within us. If we can conceive the thought of not being able to do something, we surely have the capacity to conceive the thought of being able to do it. This shift in mindset from "I can't" to "I can" can make a significant difference in our lives. However, it's equally important to remember that saying "I can" is just the first step. It must be followed by action. The power of "can" is not just in saying it, but in believing it and acting upon it.

THE VALUE OF FAILURE

"The Value of Failure: 'Why not assign the same value to our failures as we do to our successes? After all, each setback is just another step on the path to success.'" This insightful statement encourages us to reevaluate how we perceive failure. The quote "Why not assign the same value to our failures as we do to our successes? After all, each setback is just another step on the path to success" perfectly encapsulates this idea. It's about understanding that failure is not the opposite of success, but a part of it. Each failure provides valuable lessons and insights that can guide us towards our goals. By assigning the same value to our failures as we do to our successes, we transform setbacks into stepping stones on the path to success.

BEING HUMAN, NOT SUPERMAN

"Being Human, Not Superman: 'Don't be too hard on yourself, after all you're only human not a superman.'" This compassionate statement reminds us of the importance of self-compassion and understanding. The quote "Don't be too hard on yourself, after all you're only human not a superman" perfectly encapsulates this idea. It's about recognizing that we are human beings, not superhuman. We have our strengths and weaknesses, and we are prone to make mistakes. It's okay to not be perfect, to not have all the answers, and to not be able to do everything. Remember, while we should be gentle with ourselves, we should also push ourselves to reach our potential. Being human, not superman, is about embracing our humanity with all its imperfections and using it as a stepping stone.

THE HUMAN NATURE OF CRYING

"The Human Nature of Crying: 'Crying is about being a human being, it is not about being a man or a woman. So go ahead, cry if you need to, fear not.'" This empathetic statement emphasizes the universality of emotions and the human nature of expressing them. The quote "Crying is about being a human being, it is not about being a man or a woman. So go ahead, cry if you need to, fear not" perfectly encapsulates this idea. It's about understanding that crying is a natural human response to a range of emotions, from joy to sorrow, regardless of gender. It's a way for us to express our feelings and cope with our experiences. However, it's equally important to remember that while crying is a natural response, it's not the only way to express emotions. Everyone has their own ways of dealing with emotions, and it's important to respect that.

THE ESSENCE OF TRUE LOVE

"The Essence of True Love: 'To truly love is to respect, before anything else.'" This profound statement emphasizes the fundamental role of respect in love. The quote "To truly love is to respect, before anything else" perfectly encapsulates this idea. True love is not merely about affection or attraction. It's about respect. Respect for the other person's individuality, their choices, their feelings, and their journey. It's about understanding that love is not about possession, but about appreciation. However, it's equally important to remember that respect in love is not just about respecting the other person, but also about self-respect. We cannot truly respect others if we do not respect ourselves. And we cannot truly love others if we do not love.

FEEDING THE BODY AND SOUL

"Feeding the Body and Soul: 'Feed your body with nutritional food, feed your mind, heart, spirit with knowledge and what makes you happy.'" This insightful statement emphasizes the importance of nourishing not just our physical bodies, but also our minds, hearts, and spirits the quote "Feed your body with nutritional food, feed your mind, heart, spirit with knowledge and what makes you happy" perfectly encapsulates this idea. It's about understanding that holistic well-being involves both physical and mental nourishment. Feeding our bodies with nutritional food is crucial for maintaining physical health and vitality. But just as our bodies need nourishment, so do our minds, hearts, and spirits. This can be achieved through continuous learning, emotional self-care, and engaging in activities that bring us joy and fulfillment.

THE POWER OF REFLECTION

"The Power of Reflection: 'Sit and do nothing but reflect, you will be surprised how many things you will discover about yourself.'" This insightful statement emphasizes the importance of self-reflection in personal growth and self-discovery. The quote "Sit and do nothing but reflect, you will be surprised how many things you will discover about yourself" perfectly encapsulates this idea. It's about understanding that taking time to reflect on our thoughts, feelings, and experiences can lead to significant self-discoveries. Reflection is a powerful tool for self-improvement. It allows us to gain a deeper understanding of ourselves, our values, our goals, and our relationships. It helps us make sense of our experiences, learn from our mistakes, and plan for the future. However, it's equally important to remember that reflection should be a constructive process.

THE UNPLANNED JOURNEY

"The Unplanned Journey: 'Life is what happens when you're busy making other plans.'" This profound statement was made by the legendary musician, **John Lennon**. It emphasizes the unpredictability of life and the importance of adaptability. John Lennon's quote, "Life is what happens when you're busy making other plans," perfectly encapsulates the idea that life doesn't always go according to plan. It's about understanding that while we can plan for the future, we cannot control every aspect of it. Life has a way of surprising us, often when we're busy making other plans. However, it's equally important to remember that these unplanned events are not necessarily negative. They can lead to new opportunities, learning experiences, and personal growth. It's about embracing the unpredictability of life and adapting to the changes it brings.

PASSION FUELS GREATNESS

"Passion Fuels Greatness: 'The only way to do great work is to love what you do.'" This inspiring statement was made by the visionary entrepreneur, **Steve Jobs**. It emphasizes the pivotal role of passion in achieving greatness. Steve Jobs' quote, "The only way to do great work is to love what you do," perfectly encapsulates the idea that passion is the driving force behind excellence. It's about understanding that when we love what we do, we put our heart and soul into it, leading to extraordinary results However, it's equally important to remember that finding what we love to do is a journey in itself. It requires exploration, experimentation, and sometimes, stepping out of our comfort zones. It's about discovering our interests, honing our skills, and aligning them with what we love.

.

OPPORTUNITY AMIDS DIFFICULTY

"Opportunity Amidst Difficulty: 'In the middle of every difficulty lies opportunity.'" This insightful statement was made by the renowned physicist, **Albert Einstein**. It emphasizes the potential for finding opportunities in the face of challenges Albert Einstein's quote, "In the middle of every difficulty lies opportunity," perfectly encapsulates the idea that challenges often bring with them the seeds of new possibilities. It's about understanding that difficulties are not just obstacles, but also catalysts for growth and innovation. However, it's equally important to remember that recognizing these opportunities requires a positive mindset and resilience. It's about viewing challenges not as setbacks, but as stepping stones towards new opportunities As Albert Einstein wisely said, "In the middle of every difficulty lies opportunity." So let's embrace challenges, for they often lead us to paths we never would have discovered otherwise.

.

THE SLOW BUT STEADY PROGRESS

"The Slow but Steady Progress: 'It does not matter how slowly you go as long as you do not stop.'" This wise statement was made by the ancient Chinese philosopher, **Confucius**. It emphasizes the importance of persistence and perseverance in achieving our goals. Confucius' quote, "It does not matter how slowly you go as long as you do not stop," perfectly encapsulates the idea that progress, no matter how slow, is still progress.

It's about understanding that the journey towards our goals is not always about speed, but about persistence and continuous effort. However, it's equally important to remember that while we should strive for progress, we should also be patient with ourselves. Success takes time, and it's okay to move at our own pace. In the context of our own lives, this could mean taking small steps towards our goals, celebrating small victories, and understanding that every step, no matter how small, brings us closer to our goals

.

RISING ABOVE THE FALL

Nelson Mandela once said, "The greatest glory in living lies not in never falling, but in rising every time we fall." This quote encapsulates the essence of resilience. Life is a journey filled with ups and downs. However, the true test of our character is not in avoiding failure, but in how we respond to it.

Every setback is an opportunity for growth. When we fall, we gain a new perspective, allowing us to identify the obstacles that led to our downfall. Rising again requires courage, acceptance of our mistakes, and confrontation of our fears. But in doing so, we gain wisdom and strength. So, let's not fear failure. Instead, let's see it as a chance to rise again, stronger and wiser. For the greatest glory in living is not in never falling, but in rising every time we fall

.

BELIEVE IN YOUR DREAMS

Eleanor Roosevelt, a woman of strength and wisdom, once said, "The future belongs to those who believe in the beauty of their dreams." This statement is a powerful testament to the importance of faith in our aspirations. Dreams are the seeds of our future. They are the visions we hold for ourselves, the goals we aspire to achieve, and the heights we aim to reach. But dreams alone are not enough.

They must be coupled with belief - a deep, unwavering faith in their beauty and potential. Believing in our dreams means trusting in our abilities, embracing our passions, and having the courage to pursue what we desire. It means standing firm in the face of adversity, remaining steadfast when faced with obstacles, and persevering when the path becomes difficult.

FEELING THE INVISIBLE BEAUTY

"Feeling the Invisible Beauty" is a concept inspired by Helen Keller's quote: "The best and most beautiful things in the world cannot be seen or even touched - they must be felt with the heart." It emphasizes that true beauty is not always tangible. It's often found in experiences and emotions that touch our hearts. This could be a kind gesture, a meaningful conversation, or a shared silence. These intangible experiences, though unseen and untouched, hold immense beauty because they enrich our lives and touch our hearts. let's strive to feel the invisible beauty around us, for it truly enriches our lives.

BELIEVING THE IMPOSSIBLE

"Believing the Impossible: 'The only way to achieve the impossible is to believe it is possible.' - Charles Kingsleigh" is a powerful concept originally penned by Charles Kingsleigh that emphasizes the power of belief in achieving what seems impossible. The quote "The only way to achieve the impossible is to believe it is possible" perfectly encapsulates this idea. It's about understanding that our beliefs can shape our realities, and that believing in the possibility of achieving something is the first step towards making it a reality. Every goal we set and strive for today, no matter how impossible it seems, becomes achievable when we believe in its possibility. However, it's equally important to not let doubts or fears deter us, but to hold onto our belief in the face of challenges.

CONTENTMENT IN SIMPLICITY

"Contentment in Simplicity: 'The greatest wealth is to live content with little.'" This profound statement was written by the renowned philosopher, **Plato**. It emphasizes the value of finding contentment in simplicity, rather than in material wealth. Plato's quote, "The greatest wealth is to live content with little," encapsulates the idea that true wealth is not about having a lot of material possessions, but about being content with what we have. It's about understanding that the simple things in life often bring the most happiness. However, it's equally important to remember that contentment doesn't mean complacency. While we should appreciate what we have, we should also strive for growth and improvement. As Plato wisely said, "The greatest wealth is to live content with little." So, let's embrace simplicity, find contentment in what we have, and cherish the true wealth that comes from within.

THE FIRST STEP OF LONG JOURNEY

"The First Step of a Long Journey: 'The journey of a thousand miles begins with one step.'" This insightful statement was penned by the ancient Chinese philosopher, **Lao Tzu**. It emphasizes the importance of taking the first step, no matter how daunting the journey ahead may seem. Lao Tzu's quote, "The journey of a thousand miles begins with one step," encapsulates the idea that every journey, no matter how long, starts with a single step. It's about understanding that progress is made one step at a time, and that every step, no matter how small, brings us closer to our destination. the courage to take that first step, and the perseverance to continue the journey, one step at a time.

EMBRACE GROWTH

"Embrace Growth: 'Life is a journey marked by self-growth and enriched by experiences.'" This phrase is not just about the continuous development we undergo, but also about the enrichment that comes from our experiences. It's about living each day in pursuit of knowledge and wisdom, making choices that foster growth, and learning from our interactions with the world. This state of growth is a testament to a life lived fully and consciously. It's a reminder that with each experience, we have the opportunity to learn something new and wake up the next day a little wiser. It's indeed one of the most rewarding aspects of life.

POWER WITHIN

"Power Within: 'True power lies within you. With self-belief, drive, courage, and determination, you can become anything you aspire to be.'" is an empowering concept that emphasizes the strength and potential within each of us. The quote "True power lies within you. With self-belief, drive, courage, and determination, you can become anything you aspire to be" perfectly encapsulates this idea. It's about understanding that our true power comes from within, and with the right mindset and determination, we can achieve our aspirations. Every step we take today, driven by self-belief and courage, contributes to our journey towards becoming who we aspire to be

YOU
CAN
DO
IT

SEIZE YOUR POWER

"Seize Your Power: 'Nobody has more power over your life than you do, so live it with full lungs and to the best of your ability. After all, you only have one life. What are you waiting for?'" is an inspiring concept that emphasizes personal empowerment and living life to the fullest. The quote "Nobody has more power over your life than you do, so live it with full lungs and to the best of your ability. After all, you only have one life. What are you waiting for?" perfectly encapsulates this idea. It's about understanding that we hold the reins of our life and have the power to shape it as we wish. Every decision we make today, driven by self-belief and determination, contributes to our journey towards living a fulfilling life

THE BITTERSWEET PURSUIT

The Bittersweet Pursuit" is a journey of discovery, seeking knowledge and truth. It's 'sweet' when we gain understanding and 'bitter' when truths are hard to accept. This pursuit requires the courage to seek truth, the strength to accept it, and the wisdom to learn from it. It's not just about finding answers, but also about personal growth and evolution. The Bittersweet Pursuit" is not just a journey, but a transformative process. It's about embracing the sweetness of gaining new insights and the bitterness of confronting uncomfortable truths

SERENITY IN DUSK

Serenity In Dusk" is not just about the absence of guilt or regret, but also about the presence of peace and satisfaction. It's about living each day in alignment with our values, making decisions we can stand by, and treating others with kindness and respect. This state of serenity is a testament to a day well-lived and a life well-led. It's a reminder that each night, we have the opportunity to close the day's chapter with peace and wake up to a new day with renewed hope and promise. It's indeed one of the best feelings in life.

THE TAPESTRY OF CHOICES

"The Tapestry of Choices" underscores the importance of learning from our past choices. Each decision we make, whether successful or not, provides valuable lessons that help us navigate future choices. It's about realizing that there are no wrong threads in our tapestry, only lessons to be learned. It encourages us to view each choice as an opportunity for growth and self-discovery. Ultimately, "The Tapestry of Choices" is a metaphor for life itself. Just as a tapestry is woven thread by thread, our lives are shaped choice by choice. Each choice we make adds a new thread to our tapestry, contributing to the overall pattern of our lives.

THE PATH OF RESILIENCE

The Path of Resilience" symbolizes the journey of overcoming life's challenges. The quote emphasizes that resilience is about enduring hardships, symbolized by "painful rocks", with the knowledge that stability awaits. It's about-facing obstacles, learning from them, and emerging stronger. This path, though rocky, leads to growth and peace, celebrating our ability to adapt and persevere. It's a testament to our inner strength and resilience. Furthermore, it underscores the importance of faith and perseverance. It's about trusting in our ability to navigate through the rocky terrain, and believing in the promise of stability and peace at the end.

THE MIRROR OF ACCOUNTABILITY

signifies personal responsibility, suggesting that our actions are reflections of who we are. If we can't accept our own actions, it's unrealistic to expect others to do so. This concept encourages self-awareness, honesty, and growth. It's about acknowledging our actions, learning from them, and striving to improve. The mirror also serves as a reminder that our actions have consequences, and we are the ones who must face them. It promotes integrity, as we are encouraged to stand by our actions, whether they lead to success or failure. It fosters resilience, as we learn to adapt and grow from our mistakes

THE BALANCE OF BEING

"The Balance of Being" is a profound concept that emphasizes the importance of maintaining a healthy balance between our personal and professional lives. The quote "Don't be so busy that you forget to truly live" serves as a powerful reminder of this idea. In the hustle and bustle of our daily lives, we often get caught up in our responsibilities, tasks, and ambitions. We become so engrossed in our work and commitments that we forget to take a step back and truly live. This means taking the time to enjoy the simple pleasures of life, to appreciate the beauty around us, to nurture our relationships, and to engage in activities that bring us joy and fulfillment.

Thank you

DEAR LOVELY, READERS

As you turn this final page, my hope is that the words you've encountered in this book have resonated with you, inspired you, and perhaps even challenged you. Remember, each quote, each line of prose, is a reflection of life's tapestry - intricate, diverse, and profoundly beautiful. May these words serve as stepping stones on your journey, guiding you, enlightening you, and reminding you of the strength and resilience within you.

DISCOVER PERSONAL GROWTH AND HOLISTIC LIVING WITH MY PUBLISHED WORKS

Dear Readers,

Allow me to introduce you to my two books:

Inspirational and Empowering a Holistic Journey - This book is a treasure trove of personal reflections and life lessons. It serves as a guide for those embarking on a journey towards self-discovery and personal growth. The book encourages readers to explore their inner selves, fostering a deeper understanding of their own mind, body, and spirit. Published in 2024, it has been a source of inspiration and empowerment for many.

Embracing Wholeness Mottos and Affirmations for a Holistic Life" - This book provides a collection of mottos and affirmations designed to promote a healthier, more holistic lifestyle. It encourages readers to embrace the concept of wholeness in their lives, nurturing their physical, emotional, and spiritual well-being.

Both books offer valuable insights and practical advice that can benefit readers in numerous ways:

Personal Growth: The books provide guidance and inspiration for personal development, helping readers to grow and evolve in their personal and professional lives.

Mindfulness: Through reflections, mottos, and affirmations, the books promote mindfulness, encouraging readers to live in the present moment and cultivate a deeper awareness of their thoughts and feelings.

Holistic Living: The books emphasize the importance of holistic living, advocating for a balanced lifestyle that nurtures the mind, body, and spirit.

Empowerment: The books empower readers to take control of their lives, make positive changes, and strive towards their goals and aspirations.

As you delve into these books, you'll embark on a transformative journey towards self-discovery, personal growth, and holistic living. Enjoy the journey!

Stay tuned for my upcoming work, "Dance of a Fragile Heart", a collection of free verse poetry

reflecting resilience, expected to be released by the end of 2024.

www.ingramcontent.com/pod-product-compliance
Lightning Source LLC
Chambersburg PA
CBHW080532180726
48002CB00023B/2920